TYNESIDE
AT
WAR

Clive Hardy &
Paul Harris

ARCHIVE PUBLICATIONS
in association with
THE NEWCASTLE CHRONICLE & JOURNAL

First published 1988 by Archive Publications Ltd
Carrington Business Park, Urmston,
Manchester
in association with
The Newcastle Chronicle & Journal Ltd
Groat Market
Newcastle

© Copyright text and arrangement Archive Publications Ltd., 1988
ISBN 0 948946 07 5 Photographs © Copyright lenders as per *Sources of Pictures*, page 128
Production by Richardson Press

A typical wartime scene on the Tyne: four warships — Battle class destroyers HMS *Armada, Solebay* and *Saintes*, also fast minelayer HMS *Manxman* — fitting out at the Hawthorn Leslie Torpedo Jetty.

CONTENTS

ACKNOWLEDGEMENTS

Many people have helped with the research into and compilation of this pictorial story of Tyneside during the Second World War. We should particularly like to thank Eric Turner, Tommy Hewitson, Dennis Forman, Bryan Raynor, Joyce Hulme, Brian Wexham, Hugh Scrope, Ralph Thompson, Dr. Mike Willis, Nigel Arthur, R H Maudslay, Sandra Ramsdale, Bruce Jackson, Alistair Wilson, Paul Kemp, Chris Trotter, Major Don Cormack of 204 (Tyneside Scottish) Field Battery and Captain W. P. Pringle.

The following organisations and companies have lent unstintingly their assistance and their photographs and we should like to thank them: NEI Parsons Ltd., Port of Tyne Authority, Tyne & Wear Archives, Tyne & Wear Museum Service, South Shields Libraries & Museums, Cambridge University Archives, Swan Hunter-Wigham Richardson, Vickers Defence Systems, Royal Northumberland Fusiliers Regimental Museum (Alnwick Castle), 15th/19th The King's Royal Hussars Museum (Fenham Barracks), Northumberland Hussars Museum (Fenham Barracks), Royal Regiment of Fusiliers, 204 (Tyneside Scottish) Field Battery R. A. (Volunteer), Tyneside Scottish Regimental Museum (Walker T. A. Centre), The Imperial War Museum Department of Photographs, British Shipbuilders (Barrow in Furness), *The Daily Mail* and, last but by no means least, the *Newcastle Chronicle & Journal* Photo Library and everyone there who assisted us.

Clive Hardy & Paul Harris
September 1987

A photograph taken on the occasion of the Royal visit to Newcastle in February 1939 before the outbreak of war. King George VI and Queen Elizabeth open the new Medical School in Newcastle.

WAR IS DECLARED

Northumberland Street, Newcastle, is still deceptively peaceful shortly after the outbreak of war.

The formal declaration of war on 3 September 1939 scarcely came as a surprise: planning for war had long been in hand. The streets of Newcastle are still deceptively peaceful and, as yet, there is none of the bleak evidence of bombing. At the outbreak of hostilities perhaps the greatest fear was of the widespread damage and loss of life which bombing would cause and, on 1 and 2 September 44,000 children were evacuated to Cumberland, Northumberland and North Yorkshire. The anticipated onslaught, voiced by Baldwin in his gloomy prediction, "The bomber will always get through", failed to develop and, by 21 October, 11,000 had returned to Newcastle. Nevertheless after orderly rehearsals, the actual evacuation was a mira-

cle of organisation and went far more smoothly than might have been expected.

There were plenty of willing recruits, the bitterness of the First War seemed long ago and young men were eager for a crack at the Hun.

The initial atmosphere of drama and excitement produced by the activity of evacuation, air raid tests and recruiting subsided as the 'Phoney War' set in. For civilians, indeed, there was little evidence of war. Although, as Newcastle nurse Brenda McBryde notes in *A Nurse's War* (London, 1979), "barrage balloons like fat silver fishes rose giddily over the shipyards on the Tyne" the skies were not filled with the anticipated hordes of raiding bombers.

A couple of jolly Jack Tars in Northumberland Street.

Grey Street at the Theatre Royal.

Note the blackout hoods which have now appeared on the vehicles in Northumberland Street.

Shoppers queue for fresh mushrooms at the corner of Clayton Street: the price is 1/6d per pound.

Two days after the outbreak of war and young men from all over the North East wait to enlist outside Maple Street Recruiting Office.

"REPAIR SQUAD, PLEASE!"

" NOW! WHERE'S THAT BLOKE HITLER !!"

At the end of August 1939 there were rehearsals for mass evacuation. These are pupils at Cowgate Schools, Newcastle.

North Evacuees
Ask for Chips and Beer

EVACUATED CHILDREN IN THE NORTH RECEPTION AREAS ARE ASKING FOR FISH AND CHIPS, AND BEER OR STOUT.

This declaration was made at the annual meeting in Newcastle yesterday of the Newcastle, Gateshead and district Band of Hope Union by Mr. Frank J. Taylor, organising secretary.

Lady Trevelyan, President of the Union, who presided, stated that she was shocked to hear a story concerning an evacuated child in the South of England who, on arrival at his billet, was asked by the hostess: " Would you like some biscuits, dear? "

" Biscuits? " the boy replied. " What I want is beer and chips. That's what I get at home "

UNION SCHEME
Mr. Taylor declared that he had

Evacuation rehearsal, August 29. All the children carry gas masks in cardboard boxes.

The real thing. 3 September and children evacuated from Tyneside — sporting luggage labels for indentification and boxes with gasmasks — arrive at a reception area in Egremont, Cumberland.

The caption to this picture at the time was "They face the future with courage". Children and mothers leave for the country — an unknown entity at the time.

These evacuated children from Cowgate, Newcastle, appear happy with their new surroundings at Hexham.

Newcastle schoolchildren arrive at the Archbold Hall, Wooler, after evacuation from the city.

Wallsend children from Richardson Dees School set out for Ponteland.

Evacuation from Wallsend.

Mothers and young children from Percy Main wait for their evacuation train.

Children of All Saints' School, Gateshead, arrive at Gateshead Station for evacuation.

South Shields mothers and young children.

CIVIL DEFENCE

In August 1939 these residents of Links Avenue, Monkseaton, got together and constructed their own communal air raid shelter.

The establishment of ARP arose out of Cabinet approval in 1935 for the spending of £100,000 on planning for the contingency of war. It was widely expected that aerial bombardment would start within hours, if not minutes, of the outbreak of war. By the end of 1938 1.4 million people had joined ARP in the wake of the Munich Crisis.

Most ARPs were Wardens whose job it was at the beginning of the war to enforce the blackout and then, later, to judge the extent and type of any damage in their particular area so that the local Control Centre could despatch appropriate rescue services. The local knowledge of the Wardens was deemed to be vital in getting survivors out as rapidly as possible. Once out, it was the further duty of the Warden to get survivors to a shelter or Rest Centre. More than 90% of the Wardens were part-timers and around 20% were women.

Under the direction of the Control Centre were First Aid parties and Rescue Men. ARP also embraced the Womens' Voluntary Service who manned canteens and Rest Centres.

The most important ARP work was preventative as in evacuation and the use of shelters. In advance of the outbreak of war, Anderson shelters were distributed to Tynesiders. The prefabricated steel walls were sunk three feet into the ground and the roof was covered with the excavated earth. Hardly a thing of beauty, but many people did their best to absorb these new and unwelcome structures into their gardens. Although subject to flooding, the Anderson was relatively effective and protected against all but a direct hit. Nevertheless, many people did not bother to instal their shelters. A report by South Shields ARP Committee issued a month after the outbreak of war stated: "In a number of cases the householders have neglected to erect the shelters and steps are being taken to recover the shelters and reissue them".

A simple but remarkably effective shelter was the Morrison which could be accommodated where there was no garden or backyard. Others had the use of communal surface or underground shelters although these were generally unpopular as they tended to be crowded and smelly. Many people preferred to take their chance in the privacy of their own homes, underneath the stairs or the kitchen table.

The threat of gas attack was regarded as real at the beginning of the war and there were many ARP exercises in which the dreaded gas masks had to be donned. Many people resented having to carry them around. With the outbreak of war it became necessary to carry one to gain admission to any place of entertainment. A Newcastle cinema manager claimed that after performances his cinema was littered with impromptu 'containers' holding half bricks and waste paper used to get entry!

February 1939 and a group of curious youngsters watch the delivery of the first consignment of Anderson shelters in the Two Ball Lonnen area.

A family at Two Ball Lonnen inspects its newly installed air raid shelter in March 1939.

The Anderson shelter was not the prettiest of things to have at the bottom of your garden. But this is how one household on the Condercum Estate dealt with the problem!

Mr J Brown of Morrison Street, Gateshead, proudly shows off his camouflage handiwork. He also made special furniture to go inside his shelter.

Later in the war, the indoor 'table', or Morrison, Shelter was introduced (February 1941). Occupants of the house retired to the cage-like shelter at night.

By day the top of the shelter serves as a practical dining table — although it may not have won any design awards!

Work in progress on an underground shelter in Noble Street.

A surface shelter in Scotswood Road.

Pre-war ARP exercises in Scotswood Road area, February 1939. The two sinister figures are on an gas exercise complete with respirators, decontamination suits, wellingtons and rescue equipment.

The *Evening Chronicle* decontamination squad (1940).

UNIFORM FOR ALL A.R.P. WORKERS

SIR JOHN ANDERSON, the Home Secretary, announced in the House of Commons yesterday that all A.R.P. workers are to be given a uniform.

It would cost about 11s. per person, and would be a utility garment, like an overall, to cover ordinary clothes.

It is not anticipated that supplies will be ready in quantity for some weeks. The uniform will be dark blue with a red badge and the letters A.R.P. on the left breast.

During a long speech, Sir John revealed that there were to be no wholesale sackings of full-time A.R.P. personnel, but local authorities were being asked to arrange for a nucleus stand-by force which could be supplemented by other volunteers.

FIRST-LINE UNITS

There would be certain reductions in stand-by forces, but the scope of them would not be known until local authorities had completed their reviews.

It was not proposed, however, that on the new basis, first-line units which contained a substantial number of whole-time workers should be more than 50 per cent. of the total strength. That arrangement assumed that plans would be made so that the second line could come quickly into action.

In some areas, he anticipated that an increase in personnel would be necessary.

Report of Speech, Page Five

More Butter For Germans

Germans are to have their butter ration almost doubled, the German news agency stated yesterday. The announcement adds that the new ration will be given under ration cards covering the period from October 23 to November 19.

Children up to six years of age will also receive a double portion of butter.

The Berlin correspondent of the "Berlingske Tidende," of Copenhagen, recently gave the German butter ration as three ounces per head a week.

Queen Elizabeth inspects Civil Defence workers at St. James's Park, Newcastle, during a morale boosting visit to the City.

MEN OF *COOL* COURAGE ...

Firewatchers an a city rooftop — stirrup pump at the ready (January 1941).

King George VI and Queen Elizabeth inspect Tynemouth Civil Defence units, June 1941.

Queen Elizabeth has a word with Tynemouth ARP nurses.

Hardly the easiest way to prepare food as kitchen staff at the Royal Station Hotel, Newcastle, don gas masks during an exercise (April 1941).

Whitley Bay Post Office workers during an ARP test.

HOME GUARD

Local Home Guardsmen drill, July 1940. There are not enough uniforms to go around yet.

Councillor A. D. Russell, the Lord Mayor of Newcastle, inspects men of the Home Guard attached to a local engineering establishment in August 1940.

The activities of 'Dad's Army' can now be relied upon to bring a wry smile to the lips but its establishment arose out of very real fears. When the Germans invaded Holland and Belgium in May 1940, their paratroops played a leading role and Britain also feared parachute invasion. On 14 May 1940, when Anthony Eden appealed for men between 17 and 65 to form antiparatroop units guarding installations like factories, power stations and railways, there was a tremendous response. At first the units were mainly groups of employees protecting their own works premises and they were called Local Defence Volunteers.

Within a very short time the Home Guard was born out of the LDVs and many units were still attached to places of work. Although most of these pictures show local Home Guardsmen on parade, strenuous exercises and drills gradually welded them into an effective defence force. At first there was a shortage of uniforms and equipment but these were overcome as the months went by and supplies of Canadian Ross rifles and American Tommy Guns arrived, giving cause to gibes that the Home Guard were now as well armed as Al Capone and his gangsters! Still, Tyneside Home Guardsmen were better armed than one Lancashire battalion whose armament apparently comprised of six spears! Old soldiers who had served in the First War brought experience of battle to the ranks although few could equal that of 1 eighty-year-old Home Guardsman Alex Taylor from Perthshire who had served in the Egyptian campaign of 1884—5 and the attempt to relieve General Gordon at Khartoum.

The band of the Home Guard on parade in September 1941 is straight out of 'Dad's Army' but the Home Guardsmen on parade later in the war are more suggestive of a smart and efficient force of men.

General Sir Allan Brooke, G O C Home Defence Forces, inspects Wallsend and Gateshead Home Guard, 28 November 1940.

Gosforth Home Guard members on the march — to the Royalty Cinema to see a film show, 20 April 1941.

Postal workers in the GPO Home Guard on parade at the main sorting office, February 1941.

Inspection of Home Guard at Throckley by Major General R C Money. 27 November, 1941.

Band of the local Home Guard on parade in Newcastle (September 1941).

Northumberland Home Guardsmen drawn up on the football ground St. James's Park, Newcastle, for their St. George's Day service, 1944.

THE BOOMPS

" He says he just couldn't bear to be separated from his ..."

27

Newcastle Home Guard on its last parade, December 1944, at Barras Bridge.

Newcastle and Gateshead contingent at the Home Guard stand-down parade in London's Hyde Park, December 1944.

THE BOMBING

A scene during pre-war blackout exercises, May 1939. Auxiliary firemen fight a blaze at St. Andrew's Church, Newcastle.

By the time war broke out the Luftwaffe had already made reconnaissance flights over the Tyne and had built up an archive of aerial photographs and detailed descriptions of the many important targets in the area. It is now known from salvaged records that the principal targets included the Tyne Bridges, the new Spillers' building, Byker Bridge, the Docks, Elswick Works, the oil tanks at Jarrow, Swan Hunter's and Wallsend Slipway, Newburn Steelworks and Brancepeth Coke ovens. The importance of the Tyne for ship construction and the passage of shipping made the whole area a prime target for the Nazis.

During the so-called 'Phoney War' period there were many ineffective 'tip and run' type raids, often by single aircraft testing defences or unloading unused bombs. But with the summer of 1940 the attacks on Britain's industrial cities really began. The first major raid took place on 2 July 1940 in broad daylight during the late afternoon. There was considerable damage and in Jarrow and Newcastle 13 people were killed and 123 injured and a bomber seeking to destroy the Tyne High Level Bridge hit the Spillers' factory.

A serious raid followed on 18—18 July when about 25 high explosive bombs were dropped on the city. Three women were killed, there were many injuries and considerable damage. A bomb landed in the dining hall at Heaton Secondary School and others fell in the quadrangle.

Brenda McBryde in her book *A Nurse's War* recalls the July 1940 raids, "Every night the German bombers came over. You could set your watch by the siren at eleven-thirty". Emboldened by these raids, on 15 August 1940 the Luftwaffe made a mass attack on Tyneside in the middle of the day with some 300 Junkers and Heinkels. The effects would have been disastrous but for effective action by North East fighter squadrons which brought down 75 bombers in as many minutes — without any fighter losses. This victory was important because it successfully 'warned off' the Luftwaffe from attempting this type of raid again.

There were relatively minor raids on the nights of 13 September and 16 September, mainly affecting the Heaton area. Raids on any great scale did not recommence until April 1941. On the night of 9/10 April more than 50 bombers caused widespread damage throughout Newcastle and 300 troops were called out to fight fires. Homes were damaged and Cambridge Street School, St Michael's R C Church and Bell Terrace School were destroyed. On the night of 25 April the Heaton and Byker districts suffered heavily and there was much destruction in Guildford Place, where casualties were heavy, and Cheltenham Terrace. South Shields also suffered in the April raids and the Queen's Theatre was destroyed.

There were more raids on the north east 5/6 May and 11/12 May and emergency feeding and supply arrange-

ments were made after several weeks of bombing. One of the severest raids was on the night of 1/2 September when it was estimated that more than 1,000 people were made homeless in the Newcastle area. There was a huge blaze at the LNER Goods Station in New Bridge Street which burned for almost 24 hours. There was devastation in South Shields Town Centre. In both Newcastle and South Shields traffic was forced to detour around the centres for days afterwards as firefighting and damage control operations went on. On the night of 29 December 1941 ten HE bombs were dropped on Newcastle where the worst damage was in the Matthew Bank area. Over the next few months bombing reverted to the 'tip and run' variety although there was a big raid on Teesside in the summer of 1942. Some damage was done in Newcastle and incendiaries fell on Walkergate Hospital.

But the worst was now over with the Nazi war machine fully committed on other fronts and the resolve of the British civil population unaffected by the efforts of the Luftwaffe.

Damage to Heaton Secondary School during the second big raid of July 1940.

The surface shelter is intact but the house was wrecked and its occupant killed (July 1940).

This August 1940 bomb wrecked the roadway but did not even shatter the shopfronts!

During the first big raid of 2 July 1940 the Spillers' factory near the High Level Bridge was badly damaged.

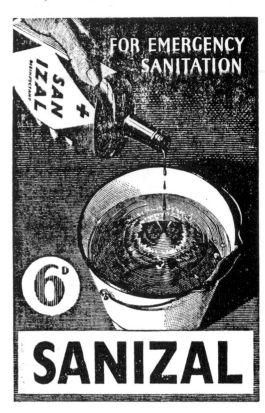

Damage caused by the air raid on the night of 16/17 September 1940.

FOR EMERGENCY SANITATION

SAN IZAL SANITARY

6ᵈ

SANIZAL

Severe damage to houses at High Heaton, Newcastle, 17 September 1940.

Homeless air raid victims, April 1941.

After several weeks of raids, units of the Queen's Messengers were drafted into Newcastle during the last week of April 1941.

On the night of 25 April 1941 the Heaton and Byker districts suffered heavily. Bomb damage at Guildford Place is pictured here.

There was almost total devastation at the Queen's Theatre, South Shields, after an April 1941 raid.

We could lose the war by Fire! Be ready for FIREBOMB FRITZ

We could lose the war by fire ! *We could. But we WON'T*. We men and women of Britain's Fire Guard will see to that.

Fire Guard work is often dull. Sometimes it's dangerous. But it's work that's *got* to be done. So we put into it every ounce of enthusiasm we've got. We watch unceasingly ! We train till we're *really* good ! We know all the awkward places, and how to get there. We won't be caught off guard as Firebomb Fritz will find.

> **FIRE GUARD TIPS. No. 2.** *It's not the fire-bomb that's important as a rule but the fire it starts. Deal with that fire first of all.*

BRITAIN SHALL NOT BURN!

ISSUED BY THE MINISTRY OF HOME SECURITY

Firmen fight the blaze at the LNER Goods Station, New Bridge Street, Newcastle, following the 1 September 1941 air raid.

Damage to flats in the City Road, Newcastle, during the air raid of 1/2 September 1941. But the clock still remains on the mantlepiece.

Damage to Queen Victoria School, North Shields, September 1941.

Following the severe raid at the beginning of September 1941 food for the homeless was cooked in the streets. In this picture, voluntary workers prepare for communal feeding.

Damage to South Shields town centre, September 1941.

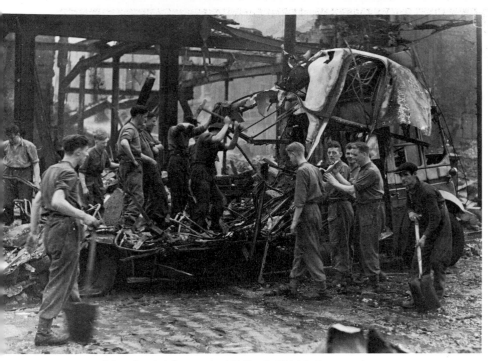

A bus lies totally wrecked in South Shields town centre.

Bomb damage at South Shields Market Place.

The Imperial Hotel, South Shields, September 30 1941.

Eyes down for an unexploded bomb in Newcastle.

All that was left of the east side of Market Place, South Shields, after the raid of 30 September 1941. Croftons the drapers on the corner of King Street is but a shell (extreme right) while in front of it soldiers examine the wreckage of a Corporation bus. ▼

▲ Serious bomb damage at Matthew Bank, Newcastle, 29 December 1941.

Extensive damage at Matthew Bank.

Clearing up at Matthew Bank.

These pictures were not released for publication by the censor at the time: the devastation at North Shields Gasworks purifying plant; salvaged possessions heaped outside wrecked homes at The Oval, St. Anthony's, Newcastle;

All Will Be Trained to Fire Guard

COMPULSORY training for fire guards was announced by Miss Ellen Wilkinson, Parliamentary Secretary to the Ministry of Home Security, in a speech at Newcastle yesterday.

The scheme will apply to fire guards serving under the local authority and also to those at business and Government premises.

But the training will not be an extra liability, Miss Wilkinson pointed out. It will take place during the 48 hours of part-time service a month.

The recent "Baedeker" raids, said Miss Wilkinson, had shown very clearly how vital a part fire guards could play when an incendiary attack was made on a town.

"The National Fire Service," she went on, "naturally concentrate on the big fires that break out, and it then depends on the fire guards alone whether other serious fires start or whether this is prevented."

FIRE GUARDS get ready! FIREBOMB FRITZ is coming

Men and women of Britain's Fire Guard *will* be ready. Ready because during quiet times we train and practise, every day learning to do our job better. We're not asking for trouble, but we'll meet it properly when it does come.

FIRE GUARD TIPS.
No. 8 Don't enter a burning building or room unless you have something to attack the fire with. Fire thrives at night as far as possible. Fire thrives on draughts or fresh air.
No. 9 Keep all doors and windows shut
10 If a burning room gets too hot for you, shut the door as you retreat. It cuts off the air supply. Besides, a door is a good fire stop.

BURN BRITAIN

BRITAIN SHALL NOT BURN!

ISSUED BY THE MINISTRY OF HOME SECURITY

The interior of St. Michael's Church, Newcastle, after the April 1941 raid.

TYNESIDE AT WAR

For those on the home front there was much emphasis on morale boosting activities like salvage collection, fund-raising and the exercise of general economies. Much of the salvage collected was quite useless to the war effort but the psychological effects were probably valuable — everybody could be seen to be making sacrifices and a contribution to the war effort in a very tangible way. Pots and pans were surrendered for transmogrification into Spitfires and garden railings (many unreplaced to this day) were cut down to make into battleships. People were encouraged to 'Dig for Victory' and parks were ploughed up to make way for allotments.

Buses had bumpers, fenders and mudguards painted white so as to stand out in the ill-lit blackout conditions, their headlamps masked and interior lighting reduced to a minimum.

As if the depredations of war were not enough, the winter of 1940—41 was particularly savage with great snowstorms in the February.

The North East was particularly delighted with the news of the release of British merchant seamen from the hell of the German prison ship *Altmark* in Jocssingfjord, Norway, for there were dozens of local men liberated.

Appropriately they were liberated by officers and crewmen of HMS *Cossack*, built on the Tyne. William Curtis, a merchant seaman from South Shields and survivor of the *Doric Star* sunk in the South Atlantic, described how he had been confined below decks for over a fortnight: "They would not let us see anything. There was very little food . . . The skipper was a tyrant".

Campaigns to raise war funds were loyally supported by Tynesiders through events like War Weapons Week and the Spitfire Fund.

More than 100,000 farm workers left the land before 1940 to join the forces and, by 1944, 80,000 women had joined the Womens' Land Army. After basic training they went off to farms in their smart uniform of corduroy breeches, leggings and green jumpers, topped off with a khaki broad-rimmed hat.

Following the raids of July 1940, many of the children previously evacuated and then returned to Newcastle and the north east, were hurriedly despatched off again and, later in the war, Newcastle provided a safe haven for London children fleeing from the flying bombs.

Members of Heaton Social Service Knitting Party hard at work knitting clothes for men on active service, pictured at Park View House, Heaton, Newcastle.

He found piano on beach

'Sunday Chronicle' Correspondent

A N.E. Coast Town.—Sat.

OLD Joe Storm has just earned £20 in twenty minutes—by taking an early morning stroll along the beach here.

Joe is a professional beach-comber, who lives in a dere-lict Army hut close to the foreshore and watches to see what the tide brings in.

Thanks to the war, he and many other beachcombers are to-day reaping small fortunes almost daily.

In this case, it was a batch of kapok bales—probably from some torpedoed ship—that produced the £20 for Joe.

Every cargo Joe and his colleagues salvage from the beach is handed over to the local Receiver of Wrecks, who pays them a good percentage for their finds.

Scrap Metals Week of July 1940 turned up some real oddities including this gun from the First War.

Children of Temple Green, Gateshead together with the scrap they collected — the gramophone horn would now be worth a small fortune!

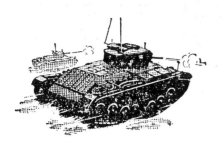

Iron Might

The iron you are asked to collect for armament manufacture will help to build the *iron might* essential to the victorious outcome of the war. So collect all things made of iron you can possibly do without and send them where they will help to give the United Nations the strength to win.

Issued by the Iron Jelloid Co. Ltd., who ask your indulgence in regard to any difficulty you may have in obtaining Iron 'Jelloids' which, for the time being, are available only in limited quantities of the 1/4 size. Price includes Purchase Tax.

It was reported in August 1940 that a hundred householders in Oakhurst Terrace, Benton, had given their garden railings to help in the drive for scrap iron.

Salvage of waste paper at Newcastle Corporation Cleansing Department for despatch to the paper mills for repulping.

What do I do . . .

to comply with the new Waste Paper Order?

I never forget that it is now an offence to burn or throw away waste paper or cardboard or mix it with refuse. I remember to leave my bus and tram tickets in the receptacle provided, or leave them on the seat.

I use only greasy paper for lighting fires. In short, I save every scrap, however small it seems.

I realise that the half-million tons of paper wasted since the war began would, if saved, have freed over a hundred ships — and released their convoys for other jobs.

And it would have made vast quantities of useful war material.

Cut this out—and keep it!

WANTED! PAPER METAL · BONES

PUT THEM OUT CAREFULLY

THEY WILL BE COLLECTED

THEY WILL BE USED

DO YOUR BIT!

CARRY ON THE GOOD WORK!

Thousands of tons of war material have already been made from scrap paper, metal and bones, collected from the homes of Britain.

Keep at it, Housewives, to-day and every day. Do *your* bit by saving every scrap—

In a bid to beat petrol shortages many buses were fitted with ungainly looking gas fuel bags. Some towed their own generator units, others used town gas but the efforts were not particularly successful.

Petrol Up To 1s. 9½d. Today

By the City Editor

THE price of pool motor spirit is raised today by 1½d. a gallon to 1s. 9½d.—the highest price for 15 years—with the usual surcharges for North and West Scotland, etc. The Government has agreed to the increase, which follows an earlier rise of 2d. a gallon made on October 17.

In a statement issued last night the Petroleum Board, the voluntary organisation of petrol and benzol distributors established at the outset of the war, says that the increase is necessary to offset the increased costs of importing and distributing petrol to which the war has given rise.

The last advance in the retail price of petrol only partly compensated for this rise in costs.

YOUR NEW 'RATION BOOK

HOW TO REGISTER WITH THE SHOPS

The new Ration Books are now being distributed. As soon as you receive your new Book you must fill in the particulars as explained below, and then take the Book to the shops for fresh Registration. It has been found possible to allow *immediate* Registration, and the sooner you register the better.

PLOUGH NOW! *by day and night*

GROW FOOD FOR THE NATION
FEEDING STUFFS FOR YOUR FARMS
KEEP OUR SHIPS AND MONEY FREE
FOR BUYING VITAL ARMS

★THE PRIME MINISTER TO FARMERS AND WORKERS—

ONE HUNDRED THOUSAND vegetarians in Great Britain can't and won't be starved by war-time rationing.

The Ministry of Food has agreed to permit vegetarians to exchange their meat tickets for extra allowances of butter and margarine.

Exact amount of the allowance has not yet been fixed, but in the last war it was equivalent to a 50 per cent. increase.

...rks were ploughed up to produce food.
...ere a tractor gets to work on Hodgkin
...rk, Newcastle.

The February 1941 snowstorm is still remembered to this day. This picture was taken outside Arthur's Hill police station, Westgate Road.

Newcastle came to a standstill. People making their way to work in Barras Bridge.

The paralysis brought about by the snow was so great that the censor did not allow publication of photographs for two weeks.

This tank — on a works test — rescued a bus in the blizzard.

A picture at the civic welcome by the Mayor of Jarrow to merchant seamen who were held captive aboard the Nazi prison ship *Altmark* (February 1940).

Tynesiders from the *Altmark* arrive home. Left to right: Thomas Hunter of Shiremoor; Mrs Woodman with her husband; Mr G Beattie; and (centre rear) Raymond Atkinson of North Shields.

The notorious "hellship" *Altmark* held fast in the ice of a Norwegian fjord where she was boarded by cutlass-wielding officers and crew of HMS *Cossack* who liberated the enchained prisoners from the bowels of the ship.

Captured Nazi planes were often put on display to raise war funds. This Messerschmitt fighter went on exhibition at Derwent Park, Annfield Plain, to raise money for the Spitfire Fund (October 1940).

EVERYONE! Get Ready for

TYNESIDE WAR WEAPONS WEEK

Throughout the country, vital industries set up 'shadow' or standby plants outside the cities in case vital facilities were destroyed. The *Newcastle Chronicle* took over a disused industrial site at Heddon and fitted it out complete with staff canteen, linotype room for setting the paper and machine room for emergency printing. Fortunately it never had to take over from the city centre offices and works but was the scene for many staff outings during the war. The picture below shows the night staff outing, 17 June 1944.

This group of land girls from Newcastle were photographed on their departure from London bound for Kent. Their smart outfits were much admired at the time.

Following the raids of July 1940, more children were evacuated from Tyneside. These Newcastle boys went to Lowther Castle near Penrith in Cumbria.

South Shields children leave for the country, July 1941. The threat of gas attack has receded and they no longer carry gas masks but are still identified by the ubiquitous luggage labels.

July 1944 and these London evacuees are pictured at Newcastle station fleeing from Hitler's latest threat — the flying bomb.

TO21255

SWAN HUNTER, WIGHAM RICHARDSON

Covering an area of 80 acres and with a waterfront of 4,000 feet, Swan Hunter's fifteen building berths had a gross annual shipbuilding capacity in excess of 150,000 tons. The Wallsend Yard was the hub of the company's shipbuilding activity; the Neptune Yard was the site of the engine works where marine oil engines, marine steam turbines, Bauer-Wach exhaust turbines, and reciprocating steam engines were manufactured.

Naval rearmament and a government backed scrap and build scheme for ship owners led to an increase in orders from 1935 onwards. By March 1940 work in progress at the Wallsend Yard stood at one battleship; three cruisers; eight destroyers and one merchant ship. At the Neptune Yard, nine merchant vessels were at various stages of construction and fitting out; Bauer-Wach turbines were being built for both John Readhead & Sons and the Central Marine Engine Works Ltd; as well as machinery for boom defence vessels under construction at Blyth Dry Dock & Shipbuilding.

As orders at Swan Hunter and other Tyneside yards increased, many skilled men who had left during the Depression were traced and asked to return — women were recruited to do helpers work. The war also led to the modernisation of some shipbuilding techniques. Welding for example, though pioneered in the United Kingdom was disdained by builders, owners and rivetters alike — even the Admiralty was against it. That position changed dramatically when a captured German submarine was brought to Vickers Armstrong at Barrow-in-Furness for analysis, for it was soon discovered that her hull was of an all-welded construction whilst our submarines were still being rivetted together.

Between January 1939 and December 1945, the Wallsend Yard laid down three light aircraft carriers; one escort aircraft carrier; one merchant aircraft carrier; two cruisers; thirty two destroyers; eighteen landing craft; sixteen merchant ships, and one fleet oiler. During the same period the Neptune Yard built eight escort vessels; four landing craft; about fifty merchant ships; two depot ships; machinery and engines not only for Swan Hunter but for a variety of customers including Cammell Laird; John Readhead & Sons; Blyth Dry Dock; Clan Line, and the Admiralty

Not all of Swan Hunter's orders were large — either in tonnage or income. At the outbreak of the war the only type of craft possessed by the Royal Navy that could land a tank on to a beach was the Landing Craft Mechanised (LCM), little more than a motorised pontoon fitted with a bullet-proof steering position. Larger numbers of these craft were required and traditional yards including Swan Hunter, Vickers Armstrong and Hawthorn Leslie were initially contracted to build them but the work was soon transferred to any firm capable of assembling them. In preparation for D-Day Swan Hunter built a number of 625 ton Landing Craft Tank (LCT) types that could carry five 40 ton or eleven 30 ton tanks or ten 3 ton lorries or 300 tons of cargo.

By the end of 1944, the Admiralty were beginning to cancel a large number of contracts placed with Tyneside yards. At Swan Hunter, work on the aircraft carrier HMS *Leviathan* finally ground to a halt when she was eighty per cent fitted out. At Vickers, orders for two aircraft carriers (*Hercules* and *Gibraltar*) were cancelled at the planning stage whilst the carrier *Eagle* was cancelled on the stocks. Vickers also had orders for a battleship, ten submarines, three destroyers and a cruiser cancelled. By March/April 1945 the majority of Tyneside yards were securing non-warship orders, with owners such as Ellerman Line; Furness Withy; Alfred Holt; New Zealand Steamship, and Anglo-Saxon Petroleum re-equipping their fleets.

A pre-war photograph of patent hydraulic frame bending at Swan Hunter's Wallsend Shipyard: this technique was used throughout the war.

A pre-war photograph of the 'W' class destroyer HMS *Whitshed* launched at Swan Hunter January 1919. During the Second World War she was converted to a Short Range Escort and armed with 2 — 4.7 in., 2—6 pdr. A/A, 1—3 in. A/A, 3—2 pdr. A/A, 2—20 mm. A/A guns; 3 — 21 in. torpedo tubes. She survived the war and was broken up at Gateshead in 1947.

Laid down on 30 December 1936 and completed in March 1939, HMS *Edinburgh* and her Harland & Wolff built sister ship HMS *Belfast* were improved Southampton class cruisers displacing 10,000 tons and carrying a main armament Of 12—6 in. guns. She was 613 feet long with a beam of 63.75 feet with a maximum speed of around 32 knots. She passed into the realms of legend when she was torpedoed by U 456 in the Barents Sea on 30 April 1942 while carrying a cargo of Tsarist gold which was ultimately the object of a successful salvage operation in 1985.

Laid down on 14 July 1937 and launched 27 July 1938, the liner *Dominion Monarch* lies alongside Wallsend Jetty. Completed January 1939, she took part in the evacuation of Singapore.

A rare photograph of the ill-fated destroyer HMS *Khartoum* (yard no. 1551) at her launching 6 February 1938. Identical in size and armament to HMS *Janus*, she commenced her acceptance trials 7 November 1939 and was commissioned immediately because of the outbreak of war. On 23 June 1940 HMS *Khartoum* was ripped apart by an internal explosion and her battered hulk was beached off Perim Harbour at the mouth of the Red Sea.

HMS *Anson* (35,000 tons) was by far the largest warship ever built by Swan Hunter for the Royal Navy. Laid down 20 July 1937 (yard no. 1553), she was launched 24 February 1940 and was one of the five battleships comprising the King George V Class. *Anson* was accepted into the Royal Navy 22 June 1942 and served with the Home Fleet until 1945 when, after a refit, she was detached from the 2nd Battle Squadron to reinforce the Pacific Fleet. She arrived back in Portsmouth 29 July 1946 flying the flag of Vice-Admiral Edelsten and commanded by Captain F S Bell, who had been captain of HMS *Exeter* at the Battle of the River Plate in December 1939.

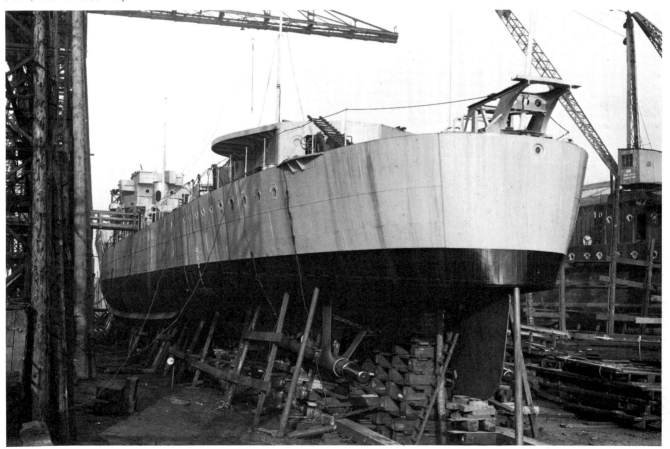

'J' Class destroyer HMS *Janus* photographed 9 November 1938, the day before she was launched. Displacing 1,690 tons and equipped with a main armament of 6—4.7 in. guns, *Janus*, along with the rest of her class, was transferred to the Mediterranean in 1940—41 where heavy losses were suffered. Only *Jervis* and *Javelin* survived the war; *Janus* was sunk by German aircraft off Anzio, 23 January 1944.

The Fiji Class cruiser HMS *Mauritius* photographed in December 1942. Laid down in April 1938, launched 19 July 1939 and commissioned into the Royal Navy in December 1940, she served with the Home Fleet until 1941/2 when she was transferred to the East Indies. *Mauritius* also saw action with the Eastern Fleet (1942—43) and the Mediterranean Fleet (1943—44) before returning to the Home Fleet and service with the 10th Cruiser Squadron (flagship HMS *Vindex*) *Mauritius* displaced 8,000 tons and her Wallsend Slipway-built geared turbines were capable of delivering 72,500 shaft horse power giving a maximum speed of around 33 knots. She was scrapped at Inverkeithing 1965.

'Q' Class fleet destroyer HMS *Quality* inches her way up the Tyne — barrage balloons flying overhead — 30 August 1942, eight days after her commissioning into the Royal Navy. She was laid down 10 October 1940 (yard no. 1603) and launched 6 October 1941. Her sister ship HMS *Queenborough* was also built at Swan Hunter (yard no. 1605) and Hawthorn Leslie built *Quilliam*, *Quadrant* and *Quail* (yard no.s 633, 634 and 635). *Quality* and *Queenborough* were amongst five 'Q' Class ships lent to the Royal Australian Navy, transferred permanently June 1950. *Quality* was broken up in Japan and *Queenborough* was converted into a fast anti-submarine frigate and survived until 1972 when she too was sold for scrap.

The freighter *City of Bristol* undergoes her acceptance trials during January 1943. Laid down 28 October 1941 (yard no. 1661), she was launched July 28 1942.

The Hunt class escort destroyer HMS *Border* was commissioned as the Royal Hellenic Navy *Adrias* on 5 August 1942. The photograph above shows *Adrias* on the Tyne 31 July 1942 and below she is shown travelling under her own steam at 8 knots, her bows blown off by a mine in the Aegean. She sailed over 500 miles like this — a remarkable performance which was something of a tribute to British shipbuilding in general and Swan Hunter in particular. A new fore end (yard no. 1735) for the *Adrias* was laid down at Swan Hunter 1 June 1944 but later cancelled. She was broken up on the Tyne November 1945.

Visit by HM King George VI and Queen Elizabeth to Swan Hunter's Neptune Yard, 18 June 1941.

The fleet destroyer HMS *Tuscan* (1,710 tons), 5 March 1943. Her geared turbines were capable of generating 40,000 shaft horse power giving her a top speed of around 36.75 knots. The 'T' class went to the Mediterranean in 1943, then to the East Indies (24th Destroyer Flotilla) and were in the Pacific Fleet by 1945. On 24 September 1945, *Tuscan*, along with HMS *Bermuda*, put into the North China port of Tsingtao with supplies for some 1,800 British, American and Russian internees stranded there. In the early 1950s the 'T' Class destroyers were converted into fast anti-submarine frigates. *Tuscan* was broken up at Bo'ness, May 1966.

The escort aircraft carrier HMS *Vindex* was originally laid down as a merchant ship (yard no. 1667) but converted whilst building. Four such aircraft carriers were built in British yards but further vessels were made in American yards where mass production techniques were used. Displacing 13,455 tons, *Vindex* carried 15 aircraft and had a complement of 700 officers and men. After the War, she returned to Swan Hunters and was converted to a merchant ship (yard no. 1783). She was renamed *Port Vindex*.

The Merchant aircraft carrier/oil tanker HMS *Empire Macmahon* (yard no. 1677) during her trials in December 1943. A number of grain ships and oil tankers were so built to meet an Admiralty requirement for additional air cover for convoys. The main difference between the two types was that the grain carrier had a hangar and lift for aircraft, whereas the oil tankers had a longer flight deck, part of which was used as a permanent deck park for planes. *Empire Macmahon's* flight deck was removed in 1946 and she was renamed *Naninia*. She was scrapped at Hong Kong in 1960.

Tugs busy themselves with the tanker *Nacella*, one of two sister ships built by Swan Hunter for Anglo Saxon Petroleum Co. *Nacella* was laid down 20 April 1942 (yard no. 1675), launched 22 March 1943 and completed her acceptance trials 3 June 1943.

The *Port Macquarie* (yard no. 1685) photographed on the Tyne February 1944. She was laid down 30 September 1942 and launched 19 August 1943.

A view across the bustling Tyne around the middle of 1944. The large building in the background is the shed where the liner *Mauretania* was built.

A smart and impressive turnout for the Swan Hunter Civil Defence staff photograph.

The 13,190 ton light fleet aircraft carrier HMS *Vengeance* (yard no. 1699). Launched in February 1944 and completed the following December, *Vengeance* served out the remaining months of the war with the Pacific Fleet. In 1948—49 she was fitted out for an experimental cruise to the Arctic. From 1952—55 *Vengeance* was lent to the Royal Australian Navy before her eventual sale to the Brazilian Navy for $16 million.

An interesting picture showing the new fore-end of the *Harpagus* being fitted to the original after-end at Swan Hunter's Wallsend yard.

HMS *Superb* shortly after completion. Completed too late to take part in the war, HMS *Superb* carried HRH The Princess Elizabeth to Belfast in March 1946. Ordered under War Estimates, she had a designed displacement of 3,800 tons and carried a main armament of 9—6 in. guns. Declared surplus to naval requirements in 1959, *Superb* was sold for scrap and broken up at Dalmuir & Troon (hull only) 1960—61.

R & W HAWTHORN LESLIE & CO., LTD

Hawthorn Leslie's Hebburn Shipyard was equipped with nine building berths, the largest capable of taking vessels up to 700 feet in length and a dry dock 502 ft 9 ins long. Builders of cruisers; minelayers; destroyers; passenger and cargo ships, and oil tankers. Much of the yard's capacity was given over to naval construction especially during the years 1940—43.

By far the largest vessel built during the war was the light aircraft carrier *HMS Triumph*, which with an overall length of 695 feet and a beam across the flight deck of over 112 feet, dominated the yard and fitting out quays throughout 1945. But if *Triumph* was the biggest, it was the 1,695 ton destroyer HMS *Kelly* that became the most famous.

On the night of 9th May 1940, *Kelly* commanded by Captain Lord Louis Mountbatten, was leading her flotilla on a North Sea sweep against German minelayers. Having left the flotilla, *Kelly* joined by her sister *Kandahar* raced to investigate a possible U-boat contact, but turned back when they received a further report that the German minesweepers they were hunting were nearby. Though the night was calm, there was mist that reduced visibility to no more than a few hundred yards. At around 10.45 pm *Kelly's* lookouts spotted "something" blurred by the mist about 600 yards off the port beam. Almost simultaneously the track of a torpedo was seen advancing towards *Kelly* but before any evasive manoeuvring could take place there was a tremendous explosion just abaft the bridge. The torpedo had ripped open the forward boiler room — killing everyone inside — destroyed the sick bay, and wrecked the wireless office trapping five men in the debris.

Kelly had a heavy list to starboard by the time help arrived in the shape of the destroyer *Bulldog*. *Bulldog* took *Kelly* in tow whilst the damaged destroyer's crew set about throwing all movable top-weight overboard; torpedoes, depth charges, anything to lighten her.

At dawn *Kandahar* came alongside to take off the wounded — it was then that the Germans struck. Throughout the day the Luftwaffe flew sorties in an attempt to destroy the crippled warship and her escort. Mountbatten not only had enemy planes to contend with — the wind and sea were rising steadily, and the *Kelly* was becoming unmanageable as tow rope after tow rope parted. That night due to a report that two U-boats were positioned in her direct palth, *Kelly* was abandoned by the last of her crew — eighteen volunteers who had stayed behind to man her guns.

At dawn on the Sunday, two tugs arrived on the scene and took her in tow. On the Monday afternoon *Kelly* after 91 hours in tow or hove-to, and after suffering repeated enemy air attacks, arrived back at Hawthorn Leslie for repairs. Testimony not only to brilliant seamanship, but testimony also to the quality of workmanship at Hawthorn Leslie. Following repairs, *Kelly* again joined the fleet. On 23rd May 1941 she was bombed by German aircraft off Crete. This time lady luck had deserted her, *Kelly* sank with the loss of 9 officers and 121 men.

HMS *Boadicea*

The 9,300 ton Southampton Class cruiser HMS *Manchester* pictured August 1938 shortly after her completion. She was subsequently sunk in August 1942 in the Mediterranean during operations to relieve the siege of Malta.

HMS *Cleopatra* (yard no. 621) was laid down 5 January 1939, launched 27 March 1940 and completed December 1941. She was a Dido Class cruiser (first group), displacing 5,450 tons and carrying a main armament of 10—5.25 in. guns. During the war, *Cleopatra* saw service with the Home Fleet (1942), Mediterranean Fleet (1943—44), Home Fleet (1944—45) and finally as the flagship of C-in-C East Indies. *Cleopatra* was broken up at Newport in December 1958.

Hawthorn Leslie's Hebburn Shipyard Loft.

The destroyer HMS *Kelly* cuts a dash at the mouth of the Tyne as she heads for the sea on her acceptance trials, August 1939. In December 1940 she was torpedoed in operations off the German coast by an MTB and although she was reported at the time as being sunk she was, in fact, towed across the North Sea and taken back into the Hawthorn Leslie yard and repaired.

After repairs she was put back into service again despite the serious damage evidenced by this dramatic photograph. On 23 May 1941 she was attacked, whilst under the command of Lord Louis Mountbatten, by German aircraft off the island of Crete and sunk. This time there was no reprieve.

Hawthorn Leslie's fitting out quays late 1941 to early 1942. Just visible to the right of the destroyers is a steam gunboat (either SGB 5 or SGB 6). These steam gunboats displaced 165 tons, were 145.75 ft long and capable of 35 knots. Their armament was considerably added to during the war and finally consisted of 1—3 in., 2—6 pdr., 6—20 mm and 2—21 in. torpedo tubes. Their complement was increased to 34 officers and men and additional armour plate fitted to the sides of the boiler and engine rooms, which led to a reduction in speed to 30 knots. In 1944 these two vessels were named *Grey Owl* and *Grey Shark* respectively. Towards the close of the war they were used as fast minesweepers. With the exception of *Grey Goose* (SGB 9) and *Grey Seal* (SGB 3), the class was sold or scrapped soon after the war. *Grey Goose* survived until 1960 after being used for experiments with gas turbine engines.

The 13,190 ton Colossus class light fleet aircraft carrier HMS *Triumph* is launched from Hawthorn Leslie's yard, 2 October 1944.

Tugs ease HMS *Triumph* to her fitting out berth.

1946 and HMS *Triumph* inches her way up the Tyne prior to proceeding to sea for trials. Insulated for tropical service and partially air-conditioned, *Triumph* was modified in 1953 for service as an officer cadets' training ship. Under the 1956—57 Estimates she was converted into a heavy repair ship.

June 1941. King George VI and Queen Elizabeth, accompanied by the Mayor of Tynemouth (Councillor Anderson) pay a visit to the repair yard of Smith's Dock Co., North Shields.

November 1941. Prime Minister Winston Churchill pays a visit to Tyneside. In the above photograph, Churchill is seen stepping ashore from one of the ships visited on a busy schedule and, below, the Prime Minister makes a shipyard visit.

HRH Queen Elizabeth on her visit to John Readhead & Sons shipyard, South Shields, April 1943. Wartime construction at Readheads was predominantly 'C' Shelter Deck freighters though the yard also built two bulk oil carriers (*Chant 60* and *Chant 61*) and two repair ships for the Fleet Air Arm (*Beauly Firth* and *Moray Firth*).

PARSONS
MARINE GEARED
TURBINES

The PARSONS MARINE STEAM TURBINE CO. LTD.
WALLSEND-ON-TYNE.

C. A. PARSONS & Co. Ltd.

C. A. Parsons & Co. Ltd. undertook a considerable amount of wartime work which was often markedly different from their usual range of normal peacetime products. This work was also undertaken in addition to the large numbers of turbo-alternators, surface condensers and transformers required for power stations and sub-power stations in this country and abroad which supplied electric power for essential war purposes.

Parsons were the main contractors for complete sets of machinery for a number of HM minesweepers and frigates. The Gun Shop alone produced over 400,000 parts including 23,700 6-pdr. breech mechanisms and 11,490 95 mm. Howitzer breech ring details.

In September 1939 Parsons employed a total of 2,176 men, 309 women and 435 apprentices. By April 1943 the profile of the workforce had changed to 2,135 men, 1,004 women and 440 apprentices. During this period 746 men and 49 women left to join the armed forces.

95 mm. Howitzer gun barrels and breech mechanisms.

Repaired marine propellor.

Welded steel gearcase

The 660 ton turbine-engined Bangor class fleet minesweeper HMS *Middlesborough* which, along with her sister ships *Harwich*, *Newhaven* and *Padstow*, were engined by C. A. Parsons & Co. Ltd. In 1942 *Middlesborough* was transferred to the Royal Indian Navy as the *Kumaon*. She was scrapped in 1949.

Bailey Bridge over the Caen Canal. Parson's Welding Shop manufactured 302 tons of bridge equipment for the Ministry of Supply.

River class frigate HMS *Cam* which, along with her sister ships *Chelmer*, Ettrick, *Halladale, Helmsdale* and *Tweed,* were fitted with Parsons geared turbines. The remainder of the class (more than 140 ships) were equipped with 2-shaft reciprocating engines. HMS *Cam's* career was brief. Laid down at George Brown & Co (Marine) Ltd., Garvel Shipyard, Greenock, June, 1942, she was launched July 1943, completed April 1944 and sold for scrap in June 1945. She was broken up on the Tyne.

150 cm. mobile searchlight projectors. During the period September 1939— December 1944 Parsons supplied a total of 56,085 searchlight reflectors ranging in size from 6 in. diameter to 200 cm. (78 in.). The company manufactured 300 mobile searchlights for anti-aircraft defence use.

Parsons' Blading Department.

Parsons supplied components for the Mulberry Harbour.

Gun Department. Shaping radii on breech block.

THE IMPRESSIVE MEASURE OF THE ACHIEVEMENTS OF
VICKERS-ARMSTRONGS LIMITED,

September 1937. The Tribal class destroyer HMS *Eskimo* glides down the slipway at Vickers' Walker Naval Yard; her sister ship HMS *Mashona* awaits her launching. Armed with 8—4.7 in. guns and displacing 1,870 tons, the Tribal class were, when built, one of the most powerful type in the Royal Navy. *Mashona* was bombed and sunk south-west of Ireland on 28 May 1941. *Eskimo* survived the war and was broken up at Troon in 1949.

Valentine tank production at Vickers Elswick, December 1944.

25pdr. field guns final assembly at Vickers Scotswood.

Valentine tank production.

Valentine Mark IIIs during an exercise in England, 1941.

Dearer Meals for Workers

Restaurant Losses

By Daily Mail Reporter

INCREASES in British Restaurant charges are foreshadowed in reports now being prepared by local authorities for Lord Woolton.

Numbers of these restaurants have been operating at a loss, and when the financial year ends in March the Ministry of Food will be faced with a big deficit account.

Losses have been due almost entirely to low-priced meals.

Some authorities have already put up prices for all-in meals—soup, main dish, sweet, and tea—from 11d. to 1s. 1d.

In Northern England a few restaurants are to be closed.

The twin 15-in. gun turret for the monitor HMS *Abercrombie* nearing completion of its refurbishment at Vickers Elswick Works, December 1942. *Abercrombie* and her sister ship HMS *Roberts* were armed with turrets removed from Great War monitors *Marshal Ney* and *Marshal Soult*, both of which had been built at Palmers in 1915.

The 7,850 ton monitor HMS *Abercrombie* (yard no. 42) was laid down 29 May 1941, launched 31 March 1942 and left the yard, eight months late, on 5 May 1943. After the war she served as Gunnery Training Ship, Nore Command, and was sold for scrap in 1965.

'U' Class submarine HMS *Untamed* left Vickers 14 April 1943 and sank on trials off the Clyde on 30 May. Salved and recommissioned as HMS *Vitality,* she was scrapped at Troon in March, 1946.

August 1937. The 9,100 ton Southampton class cruiser HMS *Sheffield* heads down the Tyne for her acceptance trials. She served with the Home Fleet (1939—40), Admiral James Somerville's Force H' (1940—41), and again with the Home Fleet until the end of the war. Among her exploits were the shadowing of the German Battleship *Bismarck* in May 1941 and her action against the *Admiral Hipper* in December 1942. In this latter action, *Sheffield*, together with cruiser HMS *Jamaica,* came to the assistance of the hard pressed escort of the Russian bound convoy JW51B, commanded by Captain Robert St Vincent Sherbrooke. Despite being hopelessly outnumbered and outgunned, Sherbrooke led his ships against a determined enemy and the destroyer *Achates* and the minesweeper *Bramble* were soon sunk. The arrival of HMS *Sheffield* and her consort turned the tide of the battle when the two cruisers scored three hits on the *Admiral Hipper* badly damaging her boiler room. Hitler was furious at the outcome of this battle and threatened to decommission Germany's surface ships and use their guns on land. *Sheffield* survived the war and was broken up at Inverkeithing, September 1967.

1. A promising young artist, Alma, studying at Art School, feels that she is doing *nothing* to help win the war.

2. Though sorry to lose such an apt pupil, her Principal tells Alma where and how to apply for a job in War Work.

3. At the Employment Exchange, Alma is told where to go for training. She is pleased to know that she'll be paid while learning!

4. Her keenness at the Government Training Centre wins her an interesting job in the war factory to which she is drafted.

Be inspired by this young lady's splendid example! Go—TO-DAY!—to your Local Office of the Ministry of Labour and National Service, and they will tell you how best to serve your country.

YOUR DUTY NOW IS | WAR WORK

The Southampton class cruiser HMS *Newcastle* (yard no. 2) was laid down in Berth 3 on 4 October 1934 and launched by the Duchess of Northumberland on 23 January 1936. The 9,000 ton ship left the yard on 5 March 1937. Women's organisations in the district raised funds to provide her with an ensign and a Union Jack and a £200 silver bell was donated by the City Fathers of Newcastle. The ship also carried a 100lb. chunk of Northumberland coal displayed above the main hatch of the forward engine room "to remind the stokers," as Captain Pinchin said, "of the arduous work they miss in an oil burning ship." During the war HMS *Newcastle* served at various times with the Home Fleet and in the East Indies where she was flagship of the 5th Cruiser Squadron. In July 1945, under the command of Captain Sidney Pinchin, she was back in the Tyne for a refit having steamed 310,000 miles on war service. *Newcastle* was scrapped at Faslane, August 1959.

The pressing need for escort vessels resulted in the transfer of 50 over-age destroyers from the United States Navy to the Royal Navy on 2 September 1940. Seen here at Palmers Hebburn Co. Ltd., (the ship repair subsidiary sold to Vickers in 1934), is HMS *Beverley* (ex-USS *Branch*) and HMS *Charlestown* (ex-USN *Abbot*). *Beverley* was sunk 11 April 1943 by U-188 south of Greenland. *Charlestown* survived the war and was broken up at Sunderland in March 1947.

SHIPYARDS WORK PLAN

Daily Mail Industrial Correspondent

MR. ERNEST BEVIN has taken a step which should arrest the fall in war production, caused by the income-tax payments demanded from workers in shipyards.

He has given more power to Yard Committees — composed of employers and workers—whose duty it is to deal with absenteeism and indiscipline.

The Yard Committees will explain to workers some of the intricacies of income tax and impress upon them the paramount need of greater output.

They will also have another function—the consideration of workers' suggestions for greater efficiency in the yards.

The launching of the battleship *King George V* by King George VI at the Walker Shipyard on 1 February 1939 was watched by many thousands of spectators. It was the biggest crowd in 30 years, the previous largest being at the launch of the *Mauretania* at Swan Hunter. Designed by Sir Arthur Johns, The King George V class had a standard displacement of 35,000 tons (average about 44,650 tons full load) and were capable of 27 knots. Their 14-in. guns had an effective range greater than the 15-in. guns mounted in older capital ships and monitors, as measured by the penetration of any given thickness of armour plate. The quadruple turrets weighed 1,500 tons each; the twin 14 in. turret weighed 900 tons; the twin 5.25 in. turrets 80 tons. *King George V* carried a peacetime complement of 1,553 officers and men and 1,900 in war.

King George V served with the Home Fleet until 1944 (though part of 1943 was spent with Force 'H') prior to joining the Pacific Fleet where, with her sister ship HMS *Howe*, she formed the 1st Battle Squadron. In May 1941, as flagship of Admiral Sir John Tovey, she joined *Rodney* in engaging and destroying the German battleship *Bismarck*. In May 1942 the battleship collided with the destroyer *Punjabi* which sank, exploding some of her depth charges against *King George V's* plating. The damage took some weeks to repair.

On 28 October 1944 she sailed for the East and, on arrival at Colombo, hoisted the flag of Vice-Admiral Sir Bernard Rawlings, Second-in-Command, Pacific Fleet.

King George V returning home on 1 March 1946 where she became flagship of Admiral S r Neville Syfret, Home Fleet. Decommissioned, she was sold in 1958 and broken up at Dalmuir & Troon (hull only).

April 1939 and all hands on deck at Vickers-Armstrong's Scotswood Works to build ARP shelters.

Pigeon-Racing Again

There is to be pigeon-racing again. This was announced last night by Sir Edward T. Campbell, Parliamentary Private Secretary to Sir Kingsley Wood, the Air Minister, speaking in London.

He said that the sport was to be restored practically without restrictions.

Sir Edward described the National Pigeon Service volunteers as already doing active service work.

Evening Chronicle: January 27, 1940

ROYAL NORTHUMBERLAND FUSILIERS

On 25th November 1941, Capt. Jackman showed outstanding gallantry and devotion to duty when he was in command of a machine gun company in the tank attack on El Duda ridge. When the tanks were held up by enemy fire, Capt. Jackman started to get guns into action as calmly as though he were on manoeuvres, and so secured the right flank. Then, standing up in front of his truck, with calm determination he led his trucks across the front between the tanks and the guns to get them into action on the left flank. Throughout he coolly directed the guns to their positions and indicated the targets to them, and at that time seemed to bear a charmed life, but later was killed while inspiring everyone with the greatest confidence by his bearing. Capt. Jackman, an Irishman, was nearly 25 years of age.

In the Great War the Royal Northumberland Fusiliers raised 52 battalions. During the 1930s the two regular battalions were converted to machine gun troops. On the outbreak of hostilities the regular battalions were sent to France with the B. E. F. The Territorial Army battalions were also mobilised. The 4th Battalion took on a reconnaissance role using motorcycles and were the forerunners of the Reconnaissance Corps.

After Dunkirk the 4th Battalion was reorganised as three independent machine gun companies. The 5th Battalion was a searchlight regiment. The 6th Battalion was converted to the 43rd Royal Tank Regiment engaged on experimental work with armoured fighting vehicles. This particular regiment formed the second-line 49th Royal Tank Regiment which saw action in Normandy.

Of the 7th, 8th and 9th Battalions, the 7th was badly mauled in France and many men were taken prisoner; the 8th became the 3rd Reconnaissance Regiment and the 9th was sent to Singapore where it was surrendered to the Japanese. The 10th (Home Defence) Battalion, and saw garrison duties in North Africa and Malta. There was also a 70th Battalion of boy soldiers but this was disbanded soon after its formation.

Corporal 'Tiger' Shaw (in tin hat) of the 1st Battalion Royal Northumberland Fusiliers at Tobruk. Shaw was later promoted to Sergeant.

Centre Left: Corporal Hall (with tin can); Fusilier Newton; Mr Stewart Moore and Fusiliers Hutchinson, Wright and Shutt of the 1st Battalion. North Africa.

Bottom Left: 1st Battalion Royal Northumberland Fusiliers marching through Cairo on their way to the English Cathedral for a St George's Day Service, April 1942.

Below: Colours of the 1st Battalion bedecked with roses. The Colour bearers are, left to right: Lieutenant W Sanderson and 2nd Lieutenant F W Ward, M.C. April 1942.

Bottom: St George's Day, Cairo. Roses are distributed to men of the 1st Battalion Royal Northumberland Fusiliers.

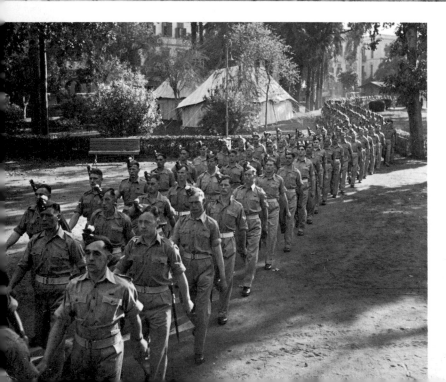

Trucks of the reformed 2nd Battalion enter Lyndhurst. The vehicles sport the Viking ship insignia of 5 Corps.

4.2 in. mortar in action near the River Gari, Italy.
Crew members are Corporal L Honeyburn; Fusiliers Quinnin and Cherry, 2nd Battalion Royal Northumberland Fusiliers.

Bottom left: The 2nd Battalion give support to Italian infantry of the Folgore Gruppo (General Morigi).

Bellow: St George's Day 1940. Bren gunners with the British Expeditionary Force (BEF) 2nd Battalion Royal Northumberland Fusiliers. The Battalion was reformed after Dunkirk.

Fusilier Hill and Corporal Edwards.

The Battalion parades through Volos.

Unidentified Fusilier of 1st or 2nd Battalion carrying his Vickers machine gun up to a forward position in the hills near Salerno, 1943.

Centre right: Vickers machine gun crew in action, Italy.

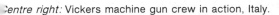

Fusilier Emps, M.M. of the 2nd Battalion takes forty winks in his slit trench at Monte Colombo, September 1944.

August 1941. Men of the 3rd Reconnaissance Regiment (8th Royal
Northumberland Fusiliers) take part in a swimming training competition held near Blandford.

August 1941. Infantry platoon of the Reconnaissance
Corps on exercise at Sturminster.

Bren carriers and Beaverette Mark I or II light
reconnaissance cars of the Reconnaissance Corps,
August 1941.

Lieutenant-Colonel E H D Grimley (Commanding Officer); Major John L Challoner (second-in command); Captain Neville Gill and Lieutenant A S Gardner confer during exercises, 1941.

Reconnaissance Corps Bren carriers on the move, 1941.

Captain Matheson praying for better weather. Holland, February 1945.

A half-track attempts to pull a 3rd Reconnaissance Corps vehicle out of the mud. Holland, February 1945.

The 4th Battalion Royal Northumberland Fusiliers can claim to be the forerunners of the Reconnaissance Corps. The 4th operated experimentally in Belgium and France on reconnaissance work, largely with motorcycles. After Dunkirk the 4th was broken up to form three independent machine gun companies.

March 1939. A searchlight crew of the 5th Battalion, Royal Northumberland Fusiliers (53rd Searchlight Regiment) T. A. in action "somewhere near Newcastle" during a training exercise.

5th Battalion Royal Northumberland Fusiliers. (53rd Searchlight Regiment)

5th Battalion entrenching a searchlight at Hamsterly, County Durham in Spring 1940.

Manhandling a Lister generator into position. 5th Battalion, Spring 1940.

7th Battalion Royal Northumberland Fusiliers mobilising at Gosforth Park.

Corporal Tommy O'Keefe, B Company, 7th Battalion at Whitby Camp 1938.

Members of the 7th Battalion Royal Northumberland Fusiliers captured by the enemy. Many were sent to prison camp Stalag 9C, camp 737, Volkenroda, where they were forced to work in the salt mines. Eventually freed by the 6th United States Armoured Division, they were rearmed and detailed to look after former Russian POWs who were burning and looting the Stalag. In the bottom picture are the Chater brothers, both of whom were reported killed in action — their family not knowing for some time that they were very much alive and prisoners of war.

Men of the ill-fated 9th Battalion Royal Northumberland Fusiliers were sent to Singapore as part of the second-line Territorial Army 18th Infantry Division (53, 57 and 55 Infantry Brigades). Many troops of this division arrived in Singapore only a few days before the surrender to the Japanese.

Originally raised as the 10th (Home Defence) Battalion Royal Northumberland Fusiliers and later redesignated the 30th Battalion, this unit found itself heading for North Africa in August 1943 as a garrison unit. In May 1944 the Battalion was posted to Malta and was still there when hostilities ceased.

TYNESIDE SCOTTISH

With the expansion of the Territorial Army in 1939, the duplicate battalion of the 9th Durham Light Infantry was authorised to be raised as the 12th Battalion (Tyneside Scottish) Durham Light Infantry. Within six months, however, the unit became a Territorial Battalion of the Black Watch (The Royal Highland Regiment). On 23 April 1940, as part of the poorly equipped 23rd Division, the Battalion was sent to France to undertake rear duties. By 16 May, however, the 23rd Division was ordered to take over part of the protection of the line of communication north of the Somme, thereby relieving fully trained units. On 17 May, the 23rd were ordered to hold a 15 mile front on the Canal du Nord but with the German advance the Division was pushed towards Dunkirk. Only 140 members of the Battalion came home from Dunkirk.

After a period of Home Training the Battalion spent a year in Iceland and on 12 June 1944 landed in Normandy as part of 70 Infantry Brigade. In July, the Battalion took part in the Ravray battle and, after further action, casualties were so great that the formation was disbanded. The bulk of the Tyneside Scottish were then divided between the 5th Black Watch, 7th Black Watch and 7th Argyll & Sutherland Highlanders. The regiment still lives on in the guise of 204 (The Tyneside Scottish) Field Battery Royal Artillery (Volunteers). A regimental museum has been established at the Territorial Army Centre, Walker.

Thought to date from late 1939/early 1940, this photograph of the 1st Battalion Tyneside Scottish shows the regiment in full marching order. Only the officers appear to be wearing kilts.

The regimental football team: Iceland.

The 1st Battalion Tyneside Scottish in Iceland.

This photograph of the 1st Battalion Tyneside Scottish is thought to date from early 1939 when the regiment was reactivated.

Members of the regiment in Stalag XXI D

The Tyneside Scottish provide the Guard of Honour for His Majesty King George VI during his visit to units of the 49th Infantry Division, 27 April 1944.

NORTHUMBERLAND HUSSARS

In the summer of 1939, a number of Territorial Army Cavalry regiments including the Northumberland Hussars were still horsed, though others, such as the Derbyshire Yeomanry had already been equipped with armoured cars. With the coming of war several regiments were sent to the Middle East where they fought from the saddle until sufficient armoured vehicles became available — or, as in the case of the Yorkshire Dragoons, they were converted to some other role (in this case to a battalion of lorried infantry). Other regiments, the Northumberland Hussars amongst them, were converted to field artillery units though they managed to hang on to their old titles albeit in modified form.

A superb regimental museum for the Northumberland Hussars has been established at Fenham Barracks, Newcastle-upon-Tyne. The collection features uniforms, equipment, weapons and photographs and is well worth a visit.

Sergeants and Warrant Officers of 274 (NH) Battery Royal Artillery at Viwgen, Germany, August 1945.

Members of the Northumberland Hussars photographed with a Valentine tank, 1945. The tank sports the insignia of the 15th (Scottish) Division, a second-line Territorial Army formation created in the summer of 1939. As part of the Home Forces, the Division manned the coastal area of Northumberland in an anti-invasion role. In the Autumn of 1943 the Division was assigned to the 21st Army Group, landing in Normandy in June 1944. The Division took part in the fighting across France and Belgium to the Maas. It took part in operations to clear the enemy from the west bank of the Rhine, crossing in March 1945 and fighting across Westphalia to the Elbe.

The last of the 'Noodles'.

The Northumberland Hussars parade at Welbeck Abbey during their summer camp in 1939. The photograph below is of No. 4 Troop (Lieutenant R A Barnett) A Squadron.

15th/19th THE KING'S ROYAL HUSSARS

In 1922 the 15th (The King's) Hussars and the 19th (Queen Alexandra's Own Royal) Hussars amalgamated to form the 15th/19th Hussars. In October 1932 the regiment was redesignated the 15th The King's Royal Hussars, arousing considerable opposition from former members of the 19th. By Army Order 207 dated 21 December 1933 honour and tradition were once again satisfied when the regiment was re-titled the 15th/19th The King's Royal Hussars.

In 1938 the Regiment was posted to York for training for mechanisation and was eventually equipped with Dragon light tanks and Cardon Lloyd universal carriers. Mobilised on 1 September 1939, the regiment was assigned the role of Divisional Cavalry 3rd Division, arriving at St. Nazaire on 4 October. During the Dunkirk evacuation, 7 officers and 27 other ranks were killed in action whilst 6 officers and 100 men were taken prisoner

The regiment remained in Britain until 14 August 1944 when it sailed for France as part of the 11th Armoured Division. From September 1944 onwards the regiment was in action in Belgium, Holland and Germany. At the close of hostilities there were occupation duties at Kappeln, Sandbech, Buckhagen and Arnis. But the 15th/19th's fighting days were not over: on 4 October 1945 they left Ath in Belgium to join the 3rd Infantry Division in the Canal Zone, Egypt. There followed tours of duty in Egypt, Palestine and the Sudan, the regiment not returning home until 1949.

World War II Battle Honours: Withdrawal to Escaut; Seine 1944; Hechtel; Nederrijn; Venraij; Rhineland; Hochwald; Rhine; Ibbenburen; Aller; North West Europe 1940, 44—45.

Guard of Honour provided by 15th/19th. The King's Royal Hussars for the visit of HRH The Duke of Gloucester to Rushden Garrison, 1941.

Rushden Garrison, Summer 1941.

15th/19th The King's Royal Hussars cross the French/Belgian frontier at Herseaux, 10 May 1940.

Re-tracking a Dragon light tank.

Challenger tank of the 15th/19th The King's Royal Hussars armed with a 17-pounder gun. Holland, October 1944.

One of the highlights of the war for the 15th/19th The King's Royal Hussars was the 'liberation' of 122 horses including ten carriage horses and three pre-war international show-jumpers; *Memphis, Zirkel* and *Turban.* D. Squadron was to all intents formed, the Wehrmacht responsible for providing grooms and fodder. The four horses in this photograph belonged to Joachim von Ribbentrop, Hitler's Foreign Minister and were a gift from the Hungarian leader Admiral Horthy. When the 15th/19th left Germany the horses were handed over to the 5th Royal Inniskilling Dragoon Guards.

The Regiment returning to Belgium halted in Nijmegen (the bridge in the background). Lieutenant Kilpatrick walks past Corporal Lucas's tank.

The Regiment on the move through a Rhineland town, February 1945.

...he 1st Battalion Monmouthshire Regiment ...adge a lift.

Rounding up displaced persons at the end of the war.

...e officers of B Squadron: Lieutenant Fryer;
...ptain Sutherland; Lieutenant Eyles; The Earl of
...rrington; The Lord Rathdonnell M.C.; Captain
...eatherby M.C.

Troopers of B Squadron inspect the remain of a Luftwaffe ME 262 jet fighter by an aut bahn. The Luftwaffe had resorted to usin motorways as auxiliary landing fields.

Lieutenant R F Eyles (extreme left) with members of the 2nd Troop B Squadron, 1945.

"Have you registered yet, Daisy?"

"S-sh! I *think* so. He's just asked me to have dinner with him."

Keep mum she's not so dumb!

May 1939 recruits march to St Thomas's Church, Newcastle, in a parade of the Tyneside Electrical Engineers.

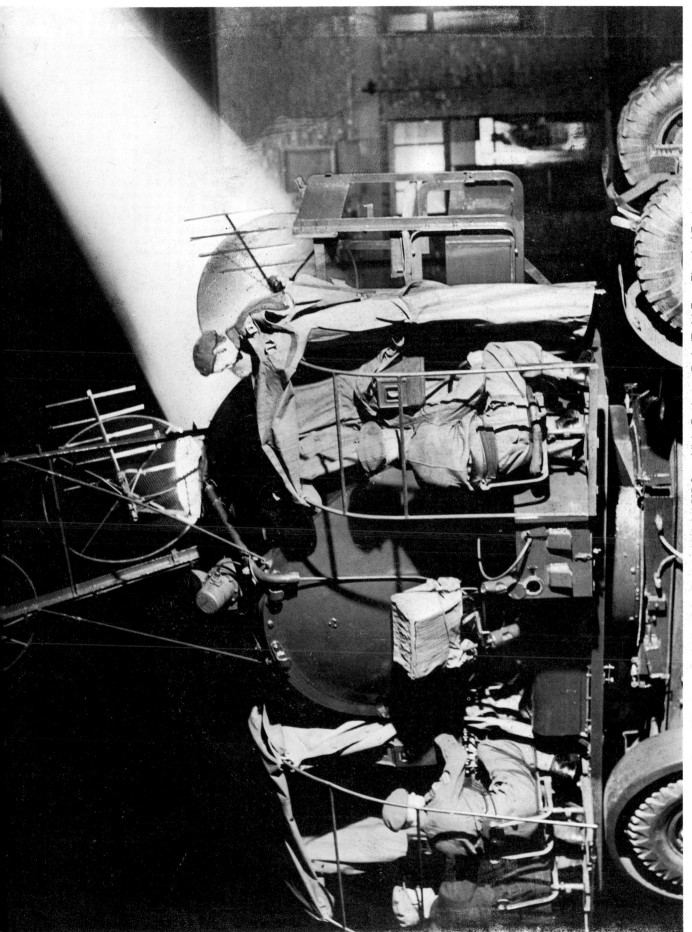

Immediate post-war photograph of a searchlight of 537 Searchlight Regiment, R. A. (T. A.) Tyne Electrical Engineers.

May 1942. Some 25—30 A.T.S. girls were employed on this mixed battery of Northern Command. Their jobs were to assist the gunners by operating rangefinders and sound detection equipment, as well as working in the Command Post.

November 1941. A.T.S. girls of a mixed battery go to action stations during a practice alert.

General Sir Allan Brooke, Commander-in-Chief Home Defences, inspecting artillerymen of the 508th Coast Regiment at Tynemouth, 28 November 1940.

A heavy calibre gun stands guard over the approaches to Tynemouth, November 1940.

Pillbox at Short Sands Bay, Tynemouth, 15 October 1940.

HRH Queen Elizabeth watches members of Northern Command's Officer Training Unit practise with a field gun during her visit to the depot, August 1940.

VICTORY!

Victory at last! Newcastle holds its Victory Parade in St. James's Park, May 1945.

The victory celebrations of the summer of 1945 were as enthusiastically embraced by Tynesiders as by all the other long suffering citizens of the country with parades, bonfires, street parties and homes and places of work decorated.

On 8 May 1945 the Third Reich surrendered and Churchill broadcast to the nation at 3.00 p. m. Almost immediately, throughout Tyneside, the flags and bunting were retrieved from dusty cupboards and bonfires were piled high in the streets. Throughout the war bonfires had been banned but the blazes that night made up for the years of hardship. The streets were decorated and great communal parties organised. The terraced rows of houses around the town were no longer dull and drab. A resident of Tamworth Road remembered: "The people in the street provided the food out of their rations and those that couldn't help turned out to watch. It was a lovely celebration".

There were Victory Teas for the children with trestle tables in the streets laden with almost forgotten treats carefully hoarded away against some hoped for day of celebration. After an enormous feed the children played games and sung songs like *Run Rabbit Run* and *We're Gonna Hang out our Washing on the Siegfried Line.*

Despite all the celebrations of VE Day, the war did, in fact, have another three months to run before the surrender of Japan. Japan was a long way away, though, and the blackout curtains could come down, street lamps came on again, shop windows were lit and signposts reappeared.

VJ Day celebrations caught many people unawares. Victory was announced at midnight on August 14 but hundreds of Tynesiders working in the shipyards and factories were unaware of the news and set off for work as normal — not knowing it was a national holiday. Those who were not turned back by train or bus drivers arrived to find works gates closed. There were parades and bonfires but not all the celebrations went so well. The Whitley Bay Bonfire was set light to by vandals 24 hours early and more than 500 people joined a premature celebration; and at North Shields there was tragedy when a young girl was killed at the minesweeper berth at the Fish Quay — during the excitement some youths took over the ship's Oerlikon gun and fired a shell which exploded on the Quay.

But the war was finally over and Tynesiders looked to the future with hope and resolve. As the *Evening Chronicle* editorial put it: "From suffering mankind there goes up a great cry of thankfulness for deliverance. It is the end of another glorious page in our island history. Time will write more, but it will not dull its lustre not add anything more inspiring . . ."

Evening Chronicle

6d BROKEN!!
Cyril Rowe

No. 21,528 Threehalfpence   A KEMSLEY NEWSPAPER   Tuesday, May 8, 1945

VE VE VE VE VE VE VE VE VE VE VE VE VE VE VE VE VE VE VE VE VE VE VE VE VE VE VE VE VE VE VE VE VE

MR. CHURCHILL IN HISTORIC MESSAGE DECLARES:—

Official Termination of the War in Europe

THE END TO-NIGHT

Warning Japan Has Yet To Be Vanquished

Mr. Churchill, the Premier, in his world broadcast this afternoon announcing the official end of the war in Europe declared:

"YESTERDAY morning, at 2.41 a.m., at General Eisenhower's headquarters, General Jodl, representative of the German High Command, and of Grand Admiral Doenitz, designated head of the German State, signed an act of unconditional surrender of all German land, sea and air forces in Europe to the Allied Expeditionary Forces and simultaneously to the Soviet High Command.

General Beddell Smith, Chief of Staff of the United States Army and General Francois Sevez, signed the document on behalf of the Supreme Command of the Allied Expeditionary Forces, and General Suslapatov signed on behalf of the Russian High Command.

To-day this agreement will be ratified and confirmed at Berlin, where Air Chief Marshal Tedder, Deputy Supreme Commander of the Allied Expeditionary Force, and General Tassigny will sign on behalf of General Eisenhower, General Zhukov will sign on behalf of the Soviet High Command.

The German representatives will be Field Marshal Keitel, Chief of the High Command, and Commanders-in-Chief of the German Army, Navy and Air Forces.

Channel Isles freed to-day

Hostilities will end officially at one minute after midnight to-night, Tuesday, May 8, but in the interests of saving lives, the cease fire began yesterday to be sounded all along the front, and our dear Channel Islands are also to be freed to-day.

The Germans are still in places resisting the Russian troops, but should they continue to do so after midnight they will of course deprive themselves of the protection of the laws of war and will be attacked from all quarters by the Allied troops.

It is not surprising that on such long fronts and in the existing disorder of the enemy the commands of the German High Command should not in every case be obeyed immediately.

This does not, in our opinion with the best military advice at our disposal, constitute any reason for withholding from the nation the fact, communicated to us by General Eisenhower of the unconditional surrender already signed at Rheims, nor should it prevent us from celebrating to-day and to-morrow, Wednesday, as Victory in Europe Days.

To-day perhaps we shall think mostly of ourselves. To-morrow we shall pay a particular tribute to our Russian comrades, whose prowess in the field has been one of the grand contributions to the general victory.

"German war at end"

The German war is, therefore, at an end.

After years of intense preparation, Germany hurled herself on Poland at the beginning of September, 1939, and in pursuance of our guarantee to Poland and in agreement with the French Republic, Great Britain and the British Empire declared war upon this foul aggression.

After gallant France had been struck down we from this Island and from our united Empire maintained the struggle single-handed for a whole year until we were joined by the military might of Soviet Russia, and later by the overwhelming power and resources of the United States of America.

Finally almost the whole world was combined against the evil doers who are now prostrate before us. Our gratitude to our splendid Allies goes forth from all our hearts in this Island and throughout the British Empire.

Japan yet to be beaten

We may allow ourselves a brief period of rejoicing but let us not forget for a moment the toil and efforts that lie ahead. Japan, with all her treachery and greed remains unsubdued. The injury she has inflicted on Great Britain, the United States and other countries and her detestable cruelties call for justice and retribution.

We must now devote all our strength and resources to the completion of our task, both at home and abroad.

Continued on Back Page

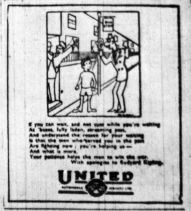

THE MAN and THE SIGN. Mr. Winston Churchill, the Prime Minister makes his world-famous sign of Victory.

Allied Forces By Air To Norway

U.S. TANKS IN PRAGUE

The two largest German forces still under arms, last night—one in Czechoslovakia and the other in Norway—have capitulated to-day.

THE BREAKDOWN in the German Command is so complete that there is difficulty in carrying out the surrender orders, but the last desperadoes are being wiped out. The position generally is:—

NORWAY.—Surrender order broadcast by German commander, General Boehme; some shooting in streets; British and Norwegian ships hourly expected; announced every radio Allied plants about to land.

CZECHOSLOVAKIA.—Germans signed unconditional surrender terms at 1.30 a.m. to-day. Prague radio stations

M.P.S BACK TO HEAR PREMIER

Thousands of people lined Whitehall to-day waiting to see Mr. Churchill on his way to the Commons to make his historic Victory announcement.

Inside the Commons there was a splash of colour—the Speaker (Col. Clifton Brown), the Sergeant-at-Arms, and the Chaplain were in their full robes of office.

But for this, however, the House bore its usual sombre and dignified appearance.

Mrs. Neville Chamberlain, widow of the British Premier who made the dramatic war announcement on September 3, 1939, sat with Mrs. Clifton Brown, the Speaker's wife in one of the side galleries. The front benches on both sides were crowded.

Lady Megan Lloyd George arrived early in a car with Union Jacks on either wing-tip and the dragon of Wales fluttering on top of the radiator.

TOOK SEAT AT 8 A.M.

Policemen kept the passages to Westminster clear. There may be some shooting for some days yet, but it will be only street sniping as the last groups of warped Nazis and Quislings are cleared.

The first M.P. to arrive was Admiral Taylor, veteran sailor of the last war. He rocked in at 8 a.m., placed his card on the seat he usually occupies and was assured of that place. Another 30 quickly followed him.

SHAEF TAKES A HOLIDAY

For the first time since SHAEF (Supreme Headquarters Allied Expeditionary Force) was set up in Paris, the notice board to-day says Reuter, carried the words, "No Conferences To-day."

In Czech hands, some street fighting; U.S. tanks reported in city.

DENMARK.—German warships in Copenhagen harbour refuse to haul down flags; clashes in Odense, resistance on Bornholm.

AUSTRIA: Marshal Tito's partisans skirmishing round Zagreb, capital of province of Croatia.

An American broadcaster from Allied headquarters said "there may be some shooting for some days yet, but it will be only street sniping as the last groups of warped Nazis and Quislings are cleared."

Norway awaiting British Fleet

The B.B.C. European service repeatedly called the German High Command early to-day

Continued on BACK PAGE

U-BOATS MAY YIELD IN OUR HARBOURS

During recent months German U-boats have been operating close to our shores, and it is a question whether they will return to their home bases or surrender in British ports, writes a naval correspondent.

The Germans probably possess two to three hundred U-boats and about a third of these would be at sea at any one time. They were mainly based on Norway.

The two cruisers Prinz Eugen and Nurnberg, both lying at Copenhagen, will be taken over by the Allied naval authorities.

The Germans also have a few destroyers at Oslo, Trondheim and Bergen, which port squadrons of the Home Fleet will proceed to ensure that the surrender terms are carried out.

Boy found dead in cabin

A 13-year-old boy, Denis Barker of Sycamore Avenue, South Shields was found dead last night in a cabin on the Holder House allotment.

An explosion had been heard a few minutes before believed to have been caused by a boiler.

A tree in the cabin had been destroyed by the explosion.

Doenitz declares:

"THE NAZI PARTY HAS VANISHED"

The "Nazi" has disappeared, said Admiral Doenitz in a broadcast to the German people to-day, explaining his surrender.

When I addressed you on the evening of May 1 to announce the death of the Fuhrer and his appointment as his successor, I told you that my first task would be to spare the lives of German men and women.

In conformity herewith I ordered the High Command of the German Wehrmacht on the night of May 4 to arrange for the unconditional surrender of all German fighting troops in all fighting theatres.

"From SO-DAY, on May 8 the guns will be silent. German soldiers, veterans of countless battles, are now treading the bitter path to captivity and thereby making the last sacrifice for the life of their women and children and for the future of our nation.

"It is not known yet what I shall be able to do to help you in these hard times. We have to face facts.

Reich foundations shattered

"The foundations on which the German Reich was built is a thing of the past. The unity of state and party no longer exists. The party has appeared from the scene of former activity.

"With the occupation of Germany power has passed into the hands of the occupying forces. It depends on them whether I and the Reich government formed by me will do so it can continue in office at all.

"If I can be of assistance in this my Fatherland in this trying time I shall do so. My love for Germany and my sense of duty bind me at my difficult post until the dignity which I owe to the German nation.

"I shall not remain in my position longer than is compatible with the dignity which I owe to the German nation."

The front page of the *Evening Chronicle* announces the surrender of Nazi Germany and the end of the war in Europe, 8 May 1945.

VE Day celebrations, May 1945, and the residents of Tamworth Road, Arthur's Hill, Newcastle, organised a street party to which they invited soldiers recovering in nearby Newcastle General Hospital.

Victory over Japan brought a great Victory Parade in Newcastle. These onlookers scramble for vantage points, 27 August 1945.

Victory bonfires were a feature of VE Day celebrations. Here the residents of Frank Street, Gateshead, pile one high.

The June 1946 Victory Parade with members of the 50th (Northumbrian) Division in parade down Grainge Street.

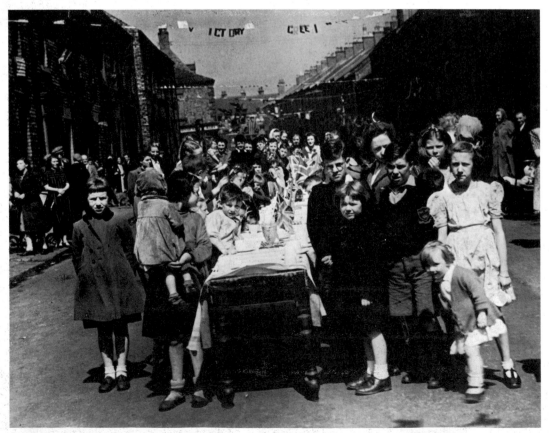

9 May 1945 and a Victory Tea for the children in Trinity Street, North Shields.

Victory Tea at Lambert Square, Coxlodge and all the troubles of war are now behind these local residents.

SOURCES OF PICTURES

1 Imperial War Museum
2 Imperial War Museum
3 Imperial War Museum
4 Imperial War Museum
5 Imperial War Museum
6 *Newcastle Chronicle & Journal Ltd.*
7 *Newcastle Chronicle & Journal Ltd.*
8 *Newcastle Chronicle & Journal Ltd.*
9 *Newcastle Chronicle & Journal Ltd.*
10 *Newcastle Chronicle & Journal Ltd.*
11 *Newcastle Chronicle & Journal Ltd.*
12 *Newcastle Chronicle & Journal Ltd.*
13 *Newcastle Chronicle & Journal Ltd.*
14 *Newcastle Chronicle & Journal Ltd.*
15 *Newcastle Chronicle & Journal Ltd.*
16 *Newcastle Chronicle & Journal Ltd.*
17 *Newcastle Chronicle & Journal Ltd.*
18 *Newcastle Chronicle & Journal Ltd.*
19 *Newcastle Chronicle & Journal Ltd.*
20 *Newcastle Chronicle & Journal Ltd.*
21 *Newcastle Chronicle & Journal Ltd.*
22 *Newcastle Chronicle & Journal Ltd.*
23 Ministry of Information
24 Ministry of Information
25 *Newcastle Chronicle & Journal Ltd.*
26 *Newcastle Chronicle & Journal Ltd.*
27 *Newcastle Chronicle & Journal Ltd.*
28 *Newcastle Chronicle & Journal Ltd.*
29 *Newcastle Chronicle & Journal Ltd.*
30 *Newcastle Chronicle & Journal Ltd.*
31 *Newcastle Chronicle & Journal Ltd.*
32 *Newcastle Chronicle & Journal Ltd.*
33 *Newcastle Chronicle & Journal Ltd.*
34 *Newcastle Chronicle & Journal Ltd.*
35 *Newcastle Chronicle & Journal Ltd.*
36 *Newcastle Chronicle & Journal Ltd.*
37 Imperial War Museum
38 Imperial War Museum
39 *Newcastle Chronicle & Journal Ltd.*
40 *Newcastle Chronicle & Journal Ltd.*
41 *Newcastle Chronicle & Journal Ltd.*
42 *Newcastle Chronicle & Journal Ltd.*
43 *Newcastle Chronicle & Journal Ltd.*
44 *Newcastle Chronicle & Journal Ltd.*
45 *Newcastle Chronicle & Journal Ltd.*
46 *Newcastle Chronicle & Journal Ltd.*
47 *Central Press Photos Ltd.*
48 *Newcastle Chronicle & Journal Ltd.*
49 *Newcastle Chronicle & Journal Ltd.*
50 *Newcastle Chronicle & Journal Ltd.*
51 *Newcastle Chronicle & Journal Ltd.*
52 *Newcastle Chronicle & Journal Ltd.*
53 *Newcastle Chronicle & Journal Ltd.*
54 *Newcastle Chronicle & Journal Ltd.*
55 *Newcastle Chronicle & Journal Ltd.*
56 *Newcastle Chronicle & Journal Ltd.*
57 *Newcastle Chronicle & Journal Ltd.*
58 *Newcastle Chronicle & Journal Ltd.*
59 *Newcastle Chronicle & Journal Ltd.*
60 *Newcastle Chronicle & Journal Ltd.*
61 *Newcastle Chronicle & Journal Ltd.*
62 *Newcastle Chronicle & Journal Ltd.*
63 *Newcastle Chronicle & Journal Ltd.*
64 *Newcastle Chronicle & Journal Ltd.*
65 *Newcastle Chronicle & Journal Ltd.*
66 South Shields Public Libraries and Museums
67 *Newcastle Chronicle & Journal Ltd.*
68 Imperial War Museum
69 *Newcastle Chronicle & Journal Ltd.*
70 South Shields Public Libraries and Museums
71 *Newcastle Chronicle & Journal Ltd.*
72 *Newcastle Chronicle & Journal Ltd.*
73 *Newcastle Chronicle & Journal Ltd.*
74 *Newcastle Chronicle & Journal Ltd.*
75 *Newcastle Chronicle & Journal Ltd.*
76 *Newcastle Chronicle & Journal Ltd.*
77 *Newcastle Chronicle & Journal Ltd.*
78 *Newcastle Chronicle & Journal Ltd.*
79 *Newcastle Chronicle & Journal Ltd.*
80 *Newcastle Chronicle & Journal Ltd.*
81 *Newcastle Chronicle & Journal Ltd.*
82 *Newcastle Chronicle & Journal Ltd.*
83 *Newcastle Chronicle & Journal Ltd.*
84 *Newcastle Chronicle & Journal Ltd.*
85 *Newcastle Chronicle & Journal Ltd.*
86 *Newcastle Chronicle & Journal Ltd.*
87 *Newcastle Chronicle & Journal Ltd.*
88 *Newcastle Chronicle & Journal Ltd.*
89 Fox Photo
90 *Newcastle Chronicle & Journal Ltd.*
91 *Newcastle Chronicle & Journal Ltd.*
92 *Newcastle Chronicle & Journal Ltd.*
93 *Newcastle Chronicle & Journal Ltd.*
94 *Newcastle Chronicle & Journal Ltd.*
95 *Newcastle Chronicle & Journal Ltd.*
96 Graphic Photo Union
97 T. Hardman
98 *Newcastle Chronicle & Journal Ltd.*

99 *Newcastle Chronicle & Journal Ltd.*
100 Swan Hunter Shipbuilders
101 Collection C. J. Hardy
102 Swan Hunter Shipbuilders
103 Swan Hunter Shipbuilders
104 Swan Hunter Shipbuilders
105 Imperial War Museum
106 Swan Hunter Shipbuilders
107 Swan Hunter Shipbuilders
108 Swan Hunter Shipbuilders
109 Swan Hunter Shipbuilders
110 Swan Hunter Shipbuilders
112 Swan Hunter Shipbuilders
113 Swan Hunter Shipbuilders
114 Swan Hunter Shipbuilders
115 Swan Hunter Shipbuilders
116 Imperial War Museum
117 Swan Hunter Shipbuilders
118 Swan Hunter Shipbuilders
119 Swan Hunter Shipbuilders
120 Swan Hunter Shipbuilders
121 Swan Hunter Shipbuilders
122 Imperial War Museum
123 Swan Hunter Shipbuilders
124 Swan Hunter Shipbuilders
125 Imperial War Museum
126 Imperial War Museum
127 Mr Chris Trotter
128 Imperial War Museum
129 Hawthorn Leslie Collection, Swan Hunter
130 Hawthorn Leslie Collection, Swan Hunter
131 Imperial War Museum
132 Hawthorn Leslie Collection, Swan Hunter
133 Hawthorn Leslie Collection, Swan Hunter
134 Hawthorn Leslie Collection, Swan Hunter
135 Hawthorn Leslie Collection, Swan Hunter
136 *Newcastle Chronicle & Journal Ltd.*
137 *Newcastle Chronicle & Journal Ltd.*
138 Imperial War Museum
139 Imperial War Museum
140 Swan Hunter Shipbuilders
141 NEI Parsons
142 NEI Parsons
143 NEI Parsons
144 NEI Parsons
145 NEI Parsons
146 NEI Parsons
147 NEI Parsons
148 NEI Parsons
149 NEI Parsons
150 NEI Parsons
151 *Newcastle Chronicle & Journal Ltd.*
152 Vickers Defence Systems
153 Vickers Defence Systems
154 Vickers Defence Systems
155 Imperial War Museum
156 Vickers Defence Systems
157 Imperial War Museum
158 Imperial War Museum
159 *Sheffield Newspapers*
160 Imperial War Museum
161 Imperial War Museum
162 *Newcastle Chronicle & Journal Ltd.*
163 Swan Hunter Shipbuilders
164 Imperial War Museum
165 *Newcastle Chronicle & Journal Ltd.*
166 Royal Northumberland Fusiliers, Museum Alnwick Castle
167 Imperial War Museum
168 Imperial War Museum
169 Imperial War Museum
170 Imperial War Museum
171 Imperial War Museum
172 Imperial War Museum
173 Imperial War Museum
174 Imperial War Museum
175 Imperial War Museum
176 Imperial War Museum
177 Imperial War Museum
178 Imperial War Museum
179 Imperial War Museum
180 Imperial War Museum
181 Imperial War Museum
182 Imperial War Museum
183 Imperial War Museum
184 Imperial War Museum
185 Imperial War Museum
186 Royal Northumberland Fusiliers Museum, Alnwick Castle
187 Royal Northumberland Fusiliers Museum, Alnwick Castle
188 Imperial War Museum
189 Imperial War Museum
190 *Newcastle Chronicle & Journal Ltd.*
191 Royal Northumberland Fusiliers Museum, Alnwick Castle
192 Royal Northumberland Fusiliers Museum, Alnwick Castle

193 Royal Northumberland Fusiliers Museum, Alnwick Castle
194 Collection of Tommy Hewitson
195 Collection of Tommy Hewitson
196 Royal Northumberland Fusiliers Museum, Alnwick Castle
197 Royal Northumberland Fusiliers Museum, Alnwick Castle
198 Royal Northumberland Fusiliers Museum, Alnwick Castle
199 Imperial War Museum
200 Imperial War Museum
201 Tyneside Scottish Regimental Museum, Walker T. A. Centre
202 Tyneside Scottish Regimental Museum, Walker T. A. Centre
203 Tyneside Scottish Regimental Museum, Walker T. A. Centre
204 Tyneside Scottish Regimental Museum, Walker T. A. Centre
205 Tyneside Scottish Regimental Museum, Walker T. A. Centre
206 Tyneside Scottish Regimental Museum, Walker T. A. Centre
207 Imperial War Museum
208 Northumberland Hussars Museum Fenham Barracks
209 Northumberland Hussars Museum Fenham Barracks
210 Northumberland Hussars Museum Fenham Barracks
211 Northumberland Hussars Museum Fenham Barracks
212 Northumberland Hussars Museum Fenham Barracks
213 Northumberland Hussars Museum Fenham Barracks
214 15th/19th The King's Royal Hussars Museum, Fenham Barracks
215 15th/19th The King's Royal Hussars Museum, Fenham Barracks
216 15th/19th The King's Royal Hussars Museum, Fenham Barracks
217 Imperial War Museum
218 Imperial War Museum
219 15th/19th The King's Royal Hussars Museum, Fenham Barracks
220 Imperial War Museum
221 15th/19th The King's Royal Hussars Museum, Fenham Barracks
222 15th/19th The King's Royal Hussars Museum, Fenham Barracks
223 15th/19th The King's Royal Hussars Museum, Fenham Barracks
224 15th/19th The King's Royal Hussars Museum, Fenham Barracks
225 15th/19th The King's Royal Hussars Museum, Fenham Barracks
226 15th/19th The King's Royal Hussars Museum, Fenham Barracks
227 15th/19th The King's Royal Hussars Museum, Fenham Barracks
228 15th/19th The King's Royal Hussars Museum, Fenham Barracks
229 15th/19th The King's Royal Hussars Museum, Fenham Barracks
230 Newcastle Chronicle & Journal Ltd.
231 Newcastle Chronicle & Journal Ltd.
232 Newcastle Chronicle & Journal Ltd.
233 Newcastle Chronicle & Journal Ltd.
234 Imperial War Museum
235 Imperial War Museum
236 Imperial War Museum
237 Imperial War Museum
238 *Newcastle Chronicle & Journal Ltd.*
239 *Newcastle Chronicle & Journal Ltd.*
240 *Newcastle Chronicle & Journal Ltd.*
241 *Newcastle Chronicle & Journal Ltd.*
242 *Newcastle Chronicle & Journal Ltd.*
243 *Newcastle Chronicle & Journal Ltd.*
244 *Newcastle Chronicle & Journal Ltd.*
245 *Newcastle Chronicle & Journal Ltd.*
246 *Newcastle Chronicle & Journal Ltd.*